Lou Ambers

Lou Ambers

*A Biography of the World Lightweight
Champion and Hall of Famer*

MARK ALLEN BAKER

McFarland & Company, Inc., Publishers
Jefferson, North Carolina

An interesting view of the New York Central Railroad at Little Falls, in the Mohawk Valley.
Library of Congress, LC-DIG-det-4a26926 (digital file from original)

U.S. Constitution—which banned the manufacture, transportation and sale of intoxicating liquor—as a comparison. Prohibition did little to curb alcohol abuse, yet it made many folks rich.[1] Bootleg boxing existed before the Walker Law, so what made anyone think it wouldn't exist after?

The key, as some bootleg promoters believed, was the enforcement of the legislation. If they could dance around compliance with the law, then it was business as usual. So, they countered with creative alternatives such as sponsorship, and if needed, a remuneration of sorts to local authorities. And, this strategy often worked. However, in 1924, and in a rare occasion, police at the Fillmore Avenue station in Buffalo stopped amateur bouts at an American Legion smoker being held at the Polish union hall. The bouts were not allowed to continue because post officials failed to procure a permit from the A.A.U. (Amateur Athletic Association). To be sure, the smoker could be held and enjoyed, but without boxing. It was a roadblock to some yet an indication of the inevitable to others.

The action prompted area promoters, as well as boxing enthusiasts, to express their dissatisfaction to local officials: Why should the fight game be in the hands of only the wealthy promoters? Why do upstate New York boxing fans have to travel to New York City to witness quality matches? Why can't the sport be used as a way to generate revenue or interest for a local cause or charity? And, what options do local athletes have in pursuit of a career as a professional boxer? The questions proved difficult to ignore.

The economic crisis that began with the stock market crash in October 1929 and continued through most of the 1930s, would force people to examine alternatives. It would also require those enforcing the Walker Law, to turn a blind eye to those trying to feed their families through pugilism.

Would the Walker Law put an end to bootleg boxing? Of course not, bootleg boxing shows continued all across New York State, and if they hadn't many folks would have found themselves on a bread line. And, talent like Luigi Giuseppe D'Ambrosio might never have been nurtured.[2]

The Process

Bootleg boxing promoters, not unlike the legitimate variety, came in all shapes and sizes, with backgrounds as diverse as cake recipes. They were entrepreneurs, prominent businessmen, athletic instructors, gym owners, and community participants, all looking to publicize the sport, and line their pockets. They were well connected, or in other words: they could accomplish tasks quickly and economically. And of utmost importance, bootleg boxing promoters also had the necessary financial resources to conduct such an event.

The process began by targeting venues—halls such as the facilities used by the Masons, Knights of Columbus, or Elks—with seating capacities that suited the type of programs the advocates had in mind. Often promoters were charged rental fees, payable by a number of methods from cash to concessions, to even tickets. Back in the 1930s, in a city the size of Syracuse, Rochester or Buffalo, event venue rentals could run about $150–$200. In smaller cities, such as Binghamton, Oswego or Herkimer, far less, about $30–$50.

To ensure a boxing card wouldn't be interrupted, promoters solicited the assistance of popular local organizations—or air cover, if you will. Bootleg battles were arranged under the auspices of: Veterans of Foreign Wars, Disabled Veterans, or the American Legion, for example. This approach benefited both parties: For the promotions, it created causes, ticket outlets and target audiences; for the venues, it drew attention to organizations and added additional revenue streams. Also, since boxing attracted primarily men—often married men, who needed a good cause to leave their home on a Friday or Saturday evening—a promotions' emphasis was placed on the association rather than the sport.

Since bootleg boxing was, well, an illegal enterprise, the local authorities needed to understand events from the proper perspective. Informing them that promotions were arranged under the auspices of many worthy causes supported the sincerity of each event. However, if an occasional financial enticement was also needed, well so be it. Suffice it to say that police intervention needed to be avoided. To counter this additional expense, promoters might opt for a cut of the venue's liquor revenue, or perhaps even provide their own moonshine.

As there were bootleg promoters all across the state of New York, many knew each other, or knew of each other. Most had either a stable of fighters they worked with, or at least a familiarity with the local pugilists. If a promoter was putting on a show, say in Ithaca, and he wanted to attract spectators from outside of town, he might opt to contact a bootleg promoter in Binghamton to contract, or entice if you will, one of his popular boxers—the travel distance between cities about 38 miles as the crow flies.

For promoters, constructing an attractive boxing card was where their knowledge and creativity entered the process. In the 1930s, a typical card included three four-round bouts, along with three six-round contests, for a total of 30 possible rounds. Impresarios often worked up in weight, but that also depended on the drawing capability of the fighters. And, they anchored their cards with solid main events to ensure a prolonged interest. It was considerable work, with challenges, or so it seemed, around every corner.

Let's say an Ithaca promoter was unable to construct a full card; he may opt to contact a promoter in Binghamton for their assistance. If a Binghamton promoter decided to provide half a card, he might ask for $25 a fighter plus transportation cost. After some bartering, he may settle for less; consequently, after the promoter's cut, a quality fighter might see a third of the agreed upon figure or less. Also, bartering between backers wasn't unusual. And, it could sound something like this: "You get me the fighters I need, and I'll let you have Tiger Perry for a main event," a Binghamton promoter might affirm. "Okay, but I also want Joe O'Dell," a Syracuse impresario might insist, "and, you'll have to promise me that you feed my boys while they are there." Such was the promotional style, or informality if you will, of bootleg boxing.

Once solid fight cards were established, equipment and referees were next. This could cost promoters about $20 to $30 per event. A ring doctor, and perhaps a few seconds to look after the fighters during an event, completed the paid personnel.

The seating capacity of a venue, and the drawing power of the boxing card, determined the entrance fees. For example: When Otis Paradise (aka Lou Ambers) was a headliner at the Old Armory in Kingston, New York, back in 1933, entrance was scaled at fifty cents for General Admission, one dollar for a Chair Seat and a dollar and a half for Reserved Seating. It didn't take a rocket scientist to realize that a promoter could make a decent dollar by avoiding all the costs associated with a lawful production.

In contrast, if the bootleg boxing clubs worked under the supervision of the state athletic commission, many costs would be fixed. For example, they would owe New York State 5 percent of the total gross receipts of admissions. It was these fixed costs that dissuaded bootleg boxing promoters from "legitimizing" their productions.

Established bootleg promotions had the additional benefit of drawing amateur boxing bouts, or unpaid pugs who would slug it out during two-minute rounds, just for the experience. As a way to reduce card costs, the bootleg promoters typically welcomed this feature. However, it was not without risk, as you never knew the caliber of fighters you were getting. The kids, who wanted to display their talent with hope of getting a paid gig, were always the best bet. Substitutions were frequent, both among the paid and unpaid fighters. Oral agreements were the nature of business; however a few clubs offered contracts.

Bootleg Hubs

Although times were tough, finding competitive boxing wasn't. Outlets for bootleg boxing, most with varying degrees of success, existed from New York City to Plattsburgh, and from Albany to Buffalo. It's also worth noting some of the names, as they will surface again.

In 1930, Garden Street Arena, operated by Ray Kohl and Frank Poole (also spelled Pooll), in Auburn, New York, staged weekly paid amateur bouts. The Arena, a converted garage only a stone's throw from Auburn Prison, held about 1,200 spectators. The promoters were so successful that they moved their promotions outside to Lakeside Park, during the summer. Known for paying top dollar ($100–$200) for main event talent, the pair commonly witnessed standing room only for their promotions.

Broadsides advertising bootleg boxing at Kalurah Temple in Binghamton, New York.

In Binghamton, things were bit different, as two promoters worked out of the same facility: Kalurah Temple—the Masonic building seated about 2,000. Eddie Edwards ran the bouts for the Elks, while Mike Minnow operated promotions for the Kalurah Legion of Honor. Rental of the facility was said to be $100 a night. Every bootleg promoter had their meal ticket, and in Binghamton it was Tiger Perry, a pugilist who fought under numerous names including Al McCoy. Perry, a licensed professional in Pennsylvania, was a gifted fighter who managed to create quite a following in the Southern Tier of New York—it wasn't uncommon for the boxer to do battle ten times in a month. Syracuse matchmaker Billy Shaw began Tuesday night shows at the Elks clubhouse in the spring of 1932. Later, matchmaker Johnny McIntyre also ran some entertaining shows out of Kalurah Temple.[3]

In Cortland, John Robson ran a bowling alley and promoted under the auspices of the local Athletic Club. His promotions were held at Fuller Hall, an old three-story building popular as a dance center. Boxing promotions were conducted on the third floor. Hall rental was about $30 a night but did not cover additional expenses such as chairs.

In Glens Falls, the Amateur Sports Club, a member of the United Federation Amateur Sports Club Incorporated, promoted shows out of the Knights of Columbus Auditorium. Close to Herkimer, New York, Lou Ambers was one of many fighters who took advantage of their promotions. (See Appendix B.)

If ever there was a town, which in this case happens to be in New York State, that doesn't get the credit it deserves for contributing to the rich history of the sport, it is Kingston. As a city in the county seat of Ulster County, New York, the municipality was 91 miles north of New York City and 59 miles south of Albany. During the 1920s, Vince Coffey promoted at St. Mary's Hall and Charlie Nettis brought shows into White Eagle

Hall. This was followed by the National Guard promotions operated by Captain John Lawson and Sergeant Jim McCabe.

Following their lead, Carl J. "Doc" Studer, an accomplished manager and trainer, brought many outstanding promotions to Kingston. Often associated with fighters such as Young Stribling and Tiger Flowers, Studer would soon add the name of Otis Paradise, aka Lou Ambers, to the list. As president of the Central Athletic Club he initially promoted amateur bouts at the new arena (Central Amateur Club) in the former American cigar factory building, along with those conducted at the Knights of Columbus Hall in Poughkeepsie.[4] His early bouts featured Willie Barrow, Buddy Emerson (Emberson), Jerry Esposito, Marty Fraleigh, Babe Lancaster, Battling Levinsky, Bud McKenna, Johnny Marello, Charlie Molvin, Vic Oliver, Johnny Raymond, Jack Sullivan, Jack Willis, and Jack J. Wright.

Otis Paradise (aka Lou Ambers), casually described as "a Filipino from Brooklyn," surfaced in the *Kingston Daily Freeman* on September 7, 1932, as the opponent of the popular Johnny Marello.[5] If Paradise needed a challenge, then he certainly found it with Marello, a hard-hitting and experienced Italian pugilist. To the surprise of many, Paradise defeated Marello in the six-rounder. By January 6, 1933, Paradise was considered a featured boxer. Assisting Studer were Harris Brown, Johnny Carpino, Joe Mitchell, Samuel Riber, and Bill Singer. Also, worth noting for the contribution to Kingston boxing: Fred Eisler, Frankie Konchina, Big Bill Freeman, Walk Miller, Manuel Quintero and Emmett Ryan.

Later, legitimate amateur boxing thrived under the sanction of the Adirondack AAU. And, it was Ben Becker, an Albany high school principal and key figure in U.S. amateur boxing that was most responsible.

Walker Smith picked up a nickname in the second bout of his amateur career held inside the Municipal Auditorium in Kingston. From this point forward, the pugilist was known as Sugar Ray Robinson. And in the opinion of many historians, he was pound-for-pound the greatest boxer in history.

Another home to bootleg boxing was Syracuse, where the Arena, run by the aforementioned Billy Shaw, and the Alhambra operated by Waldron Brower (aka Bobby Waldron) were the main venues. Both conducted weekly shows. The privately-owned Arena, with a capacity of about 2,500, featured a dirt floor that could be converted into an ice rink. The 104th Field Artillery drilled there, and the trademark aroma, kind of combination of dirt, sweat and horse manure, was tough to mask. Nevertheless, it was large enough for Shaw to make a decent buck on a sound promotion, and the rent was reasonable. The first Alhambra, built as a roller rink and auditorium, burned in 1899. The second Alhambra was built in 1900. And, at the same location at 275 James Street at Pearl Street, was multi-functional and hosted everything from boxing and basketball to concerts. It burned down in 1955. Both venues attracted fighters from as far north as Montreal, to as far south as Scranton. And, both promoters: insisted that the participants were amateur boxers, yet, did not hide the fact that the fighters were compensated for lost work time, travel expenses and incidentals. Both Waldron and Shaw wore many hats, such as promoter, matchmaker, and in the latter's case, participant. This assured each a maximum cut.

Nightclubs, although often limited by a smaller capacity, were another option for promoters. But not unlike larger venues, also faced issues. For example, Joe Netro, a name that will become familiar with central New York fight fans, was suspended, pending a hearing, by NYSAC, on March 10, 1930, for running a boxing speakeasy in Syracuse.

Details about the nightclub were not clear. Netro, who would guide Carmen Basilio to the welterweight and middleweight championships, was also acknowledged for his boxing column that he penned for the local newspaper.

In Watertown, there were two promoters. To ensure the success of their promotions, they worked together by conducting their shows on alternating Fridays and with different organizations. Although bootleg promoters were indeed competitive, they understood that cooperation was the key to their survival.

Real names meant nothing to bootleg fighters; ergo, there were fighters who fought under different aliases depending on the location. Marketing a factious identity was typically for those relying on the income at this level of pugilism, and occasionally for those dodging recognition. For serious fighters, bootleg boxing wasn't about establishing an identity—that would be done at the next level. It was about showcasing or polishing their talent, then collecting the cash.

Initially, the cost of operating as a licensed club prohibited it as a consideration for bootleg promoters. They could not afford the additive costs. It was not that the licensing fee was out of range. It was the ancillary costs, such as a minimum of $10 per fighter per round. And, instead of only paying a nominal fee to a referee, they would have to pay both a referee (often $50 plus expenses) and judges.

Legislation

Ring death, during bootleg boxing battles, always thrust the sport into the spotlight. Such was the case in 1930, when fighter Evan Gustafson, of Mount Jewett, Pennsylvania, died during an unsanctioned bout at Olean, New York. The New York State Athletic Commission (NYSAC), completely powerless in this situation, could only reiterate the need for legislation to put an end to unsanctioned shows. The Olean show was advertised as an amateur contest, yet Gustafson was licensed in Pennsylvania as a professional. Ironically, Chief of Police John C. Dempsey acted as the referee—he was under the impression that the event was sanctioned by the A.A.U.

In 1930, newspaper articles penned by *Daily News* reporter Pat Robinson, shed light on the lucrative bootleg boxing market in New York State. This investigative work, published as a series of articles, infuriated NYSAC. And, resulted in the suspension of boxing managers Leo P. Flynn and Billy Grupp, along with boxers: Elmer Cicone, Danny Dempsey, Eddie Dempsey, Sid Goldie, Steve Halaiko, Connie Holmes, Johnny Randall, and Johnny Wilson. Flynn, had suspected that some members of his boxing stable had sneaked off to upstate halls to fill their pockets, but wasn't certain.[6] More than likely he had the same optometrist as the aforementioned Chief of Police.

The NYSAC struggled with finding the correct price points to address bootleg boxing. In 1930, they cut the mandatory pay for a preliminary fighter from $10 a round to $5. They also cut in half the compensation given to referees and judges at all shows at licensed clubs where the gate receipts did not exceed $4,000.

Beginning on September 1, 1931, NYSAC handed down further reform: all amateur bouts would be limited to three rounds only (referees could not extend bouts); club fees, for a city such as Buffalo, were set at $250 a year; referees, judges and physicians must be licensed at $25 a year; referees will be paid $15 a night, while judges will receive $10; and two experienced and licensed seconds will be mandated.

The (Joseph D.) Nunan bill, signed by Governor Lehman of New York in 1933, brought all amateur boxing and wrestling under supervision of the state athletic commission. Purely amateur bouts were exempted from the bill. The legislation defined an amateur as a person engaged in boxing, sparring or wrestling exhibitions, where no cash prizes are awarded to participants and the prize shall not exceed $35 in value.[7]

The end of bootleg boxing finally came when NYSAC brought their fees in line with promoters at the local level and the Nunan bill was signed. Both actions encouraged area fight impresarios to follow organization guidelines to guarantee that their promotions wouldn't be shutdown. Although by 1935, this form of pugilism played a diminished role in the fight game, it would later be recalled for some of the great ring talent it nurtured.

forever changed the lives of those along its path.

Mohawk and Hudson valleys form the only cut across the Appalachians north of Alabama, allowing an *almost* complete water route from New York City in the south to Lake Ontario and Lake Erie in the west. Just imagine, as many did, the possibilities such a route offered. The problem was that the land rises about 600 feet from the Hudson to Lake Erie. A solution, as some believed, could be a series of locks. (At the time, technology had mastered up to 12 feet of lift.) However, it would require fifty locks, or considerable expense to the project; moreover, slow the transportation process. Even President Thomas Jefferson rejected the project.

Nonetheless, Jesse Hawley, a Connecticut flour merchant, who happened to have his wheat milled in the upstate New York town of

American author James Fenimore Cooper penned historical romances depicting frontier and Native American life from the 17th to the 19th centuries. *Library of Congress, LC-USZ62-32865 (b&w film copy negative)*

Geneva, thought differently. Hawley convinced New York Governor DeWitt Clinton that such an undertaking was feasible. In 1817, Clinton received approval from the legislature for $7 million for construction.

The original canal was 363 miles long, from Albany on the Hudson to Buffalo on Lake Erie. The channel was cut 40 feet wide and 4 feet deep, with removed soil piled on the downhill side to form a walkway known as a towpath.

To say that construction proved a daunting task would be just an understatement. Craftsmen from all over the world found their way to New York State to work with engineers—many of which were inexperienced—who developed new construction techniques to solve problems. They harnessed the power of animals and even the water itself to relieve their pain. Immigrant masons (Irish, German, Italian and more) worked long and tedious hours crafting and placing the stonework that lined the banks of the canal. Water was even redirected thanks to the construction of state-of-the-art aqueducts.

On July 4, 1817, construction began at Rome, New York, just over 30 miles from Herkimer. And, the first 15 miles, from Rome to Utica, opened in 1819. It wasn't an impressive time frame: At that rate, the canal would not be finished for 30 years. Delays were caused primarily by felling trees, stump removal, soil movement, and the lack of labor. Increased immigration helped solve the latter, while new innovations the former. As the process was refined, the frequency of production delays was reduced—most had been a result of illness and personnel issues (ethnicity, religion, customs, etc.). Naturally, weather was always a factor.

The entire canal was officially completed on October 26, 1825, and a statewide "Grand Celebration" took place. A flotilla of boats led by Governor Dewitt Clinton aboard sailed from Buffalo to New York City. Clinton then ceremonially poured Lake Erie water into New York Harbor to mark the "Wedding of the Waters."

Igniting commerce all along its path, the Erie Canal was the economic stimulus the region needed. The canal lowered the cost of shipping and the goods being shipped. And, a wider variety of goods were reaching new markets. Trade was extended across the nation with many sectors, such as farming benefiting in ways they never dreamed feasible. A wealth of additional services sprang up not only during the creation of the canal but to sustain it as well. Although initially envisioned as a commercial channel for freight boats, passengers also traveled on the canal's packet boats. In 1825, more than 40,000 passengers took advantage of the convenience and beauty of canal travel. A steady flow of tourists, settlers and businessmen brought an influx of new ideas, goods and services. Preachers, peddlers and even pugilists took advantage of the contemporary transportation artery.[9]

However, by the late 1850s the economy began slowing down. For example: In 1857, the Agriculture Bank in Herkimer, which was organized in 1839, failed and the depositors lost 30 percent of their deposits.

While the Revolution of 1776–1783 established the United States, the Civil War of 1861–1865 determined the course of the nation. It set the moral compass of a republic determined to preserve unity. But it came with a price: 625,000 lives were lost—nearly as many American soldiers as died in all the other wars in which this country has fought combined. To this very day it is still difficult to believe that the American Civil War was the largest and most destructive conflict in the Western world between the end of the Napoleonic Wars in 1815 and the onset of World War I in 1914.

Acting on the President's orders, the Mohawk Valley raised the militia to preserve order. One of the first actions was to place a guard upon the vast Remington armory.

Francis Elias Spinner, born in German Flatts, New York, was appointed by President Abraham Lincoln as Treasurer of the United States and served from March 16, 1861, until his resignation on July 1, 1875.[10] Nearly a month later, on Monday, April 15, 1861, the New York State Legislature passed a bill appropriating $3,000,000 and providing for the enrollment of 30,000 men to assist the government. The volunteers were to enlist into the State service for two years, and be subject at any time to transfer into the Federal service.

Patriotic meetings and speeches soon filled the air from Little Falls to Mohawk. Resolutions were made as a form of solidarity and relief funds were set in place for those enlisted. By May 8, 1861, Herkimer sent six companies off to Albany.

According to sources, Herkimer soldiers saw action at: Cedar Mountain, Rappahannock Station, Thoroughfare Gap, Second Bull Run, Chantilly, South Mountain, Antietam, Fredericksburg (two engagements), Chancellorsville, Gettysburg, Mine Run, Raccoon Ford, Wilderness, Laurel Hill, Spottsylvania Court House, North Anna, Tolopotomoy, Bethesda Church, White Oak Swamp, Petersburg, Weldon Railroad, Hicks Ford, Hatcher's Run, Quaker Road, White Oak Road, Five Forks, and Appomattox.

Memorable Natural Disasters and an American Tragedy

There is an old saying: "If you don't like the weather in upstate New York, just wait a minute or two and it will change." The beauty of the Mohawk Valley comes at a price: The weather is often cloudy and wet. Averaging under the nation's mean for sunny days, while exceeding it for rain and snow, the region can be a challenge, particularly in the winter when snowfall averages about 100 inches. Understanding this, residents learned to take advantage of what some consider a detriment. You won't find a single Valley resident who doesn't marvel at the beauty of the first area snowfall. Ski resorts thrive during the winter months, as do areas conducive to trail activity such as snowshoeing or cross-country skiing.

On Sunday, March 11, 1888, the snow started falling about 3:00 p.m. and didn't stop until the morning of Wednesday, March 14. "The Blizzard of 1888" had left behind 46.7 inches of snow. The capital city of Albany was virtually shut down. Most roads were impossible to travel over, making horse-drawn deliveries improbable. And, without coal for heating, many went without indoor warmth. For generations it was the "worst storm in memory."

The Village of Herkimer lies primarily north of the Mohawk River. Numerous tributaries flow from the north, including the West Canada Creek, or the stream that separates Herkimer from East Herkimer. This tributary drains the southern part of the Adirondack Mountains before emptying into the Mohawk River near the village of Herkimer. Across the river and to the west of Herkimer lie the village of Mohawk, the village of Ilion and East Frankfort, part of the town of Frankfort. Between the latter two hamlets is where the Mohawk River begins to take a turn north as it heads toward, Utica and Rome, New York.

As everyone realizes: Water flows along the path of least resistance. On February 28, 1910, the West Canada Creek, filled to capacity, began overflowing its banks at the eastern portion of Herkimer. The *Herkimer Telegram* noted:

> It remained for an exceptional season and a particular combination of circumstances to make possible the great flood which left no part of Herkimer wholly immune, for where it did not reach directly the supersaturated ground filled cellars and basements, extinguishing furnace fires and destroying goods and supplies wherever the owners had failed to remove them in time. As stated, there had been a phenomenal sequence of weather which first put a heavy armor of ice on the streams, then covered the land with masses of snow and finally turned abruptly from wintry cold to the mildness and showers of spring. Rivulets rolled down every slope and the West Canada, spreading its branches far through the distant mountains, grew quickly to a roaring, threatening giant, and the stream it was which caused the subsequent devastation.[11]

The flood left a trail of devastation across the region. The *Telegram* noted:

> In the meantime, the other arm of the flood which had reached across German Street transformed Bellinger Street into a swift stream navigable by boats with some difficulty but too deep and dangerous to wade. The water rose to the top of the street letter boxes, turned yards into ponds and the unoccupied lots on the west into a lake. A teamster attempted to drive across the street when one of his horses missed its footing and fell. The poor animal drowned before anything could be done to extricate it.[12]

After the costly flood, the State of New York working with the town of Herkimer, undertook painstaking study to develop a plan to rectify the problem. Improvements were recommended and then made around the West Canada Creek and throughout the village of Herkimer to be certain that another horrendous flood such as Herkimer's Flood of 1910 might be avoided.

Herkimer Jail, in Herkimer, New York, is a two-story structure with a high basement, five bays wide, of ashlar limestone blocks with dressed quoins built in 1835. It features a gable roof with oval window and narrow cornice and a Federal style entrance. *Library of Congress, HABS NY, 22-HERK, 3- (digital file from original)*

On July 14, 1906, under the bold headlines of "Police Arrest Murder Suspect In Adirondacks, Chester Gillette Identified as Man Who Was with Slain Girl," the *Evening World* exclaimed:

> Chester Gillette, of Cortland, N.Y., was arrested at the Arrowhead, Eagle Bay, on Fourth Lake, early to-day, and charged with the murder of Grace Brown, of South Otselic (Chenango County, New York), on Big Moose Lake, on Wednesday afternoon last.
>
> Handcuffed to a deputy sheriff, Gillette was brought to Fulton Chain, and there the party was met by the manager of the hotel at Big Moose where Miss Brown and the man who registered as "Carl Graham, Albany," stopped on Wednesday. Other persons stopping at the hotel at the time were present at Fulton Chain when the boat arrived, and the man under arrest was at once fully identified as the one who accompanied Miss Brown on her trip upon the lake.
>
> Gillette appeared to be tremendously nervous. He admitted that he had been with the girl, and there closed his statement. Afterward he said that he knew nothing whatever about the incident.
>
> He was taken to Herkimer jail this afternoon.[13]

With this, Herkimer County officials believed they had their man. Later, it was proven: Grace Brown was murdered. The weapon used was a tennis racquet. She was struck repeatedly before being thrown from the boat she was in. Gillette's defense claimed the girl was drowned when the two were out in a boat at Moose Lake.

Morning Call stated:

> Throughout the trial, which lasted many weeks, Gillette exhibited no trait which was not purely physical. The turning point of the case was the reading of the letters which the girl had written to this

boy—for he was only twenty-three years old— when she was waiting at her home for Gillette to come to take her away and make legitimate the child which she expected.[14]

The trial began in Herkimer and created national interest. People, from miles around, were even traveling to the area where the crime had been committed to make a personal evaluation. On March 30, 1908, Gillette paid the penalty of death in the electric chair at Auburn Prison at fourteen minutes after 6 o'clock in the morning. That very morning, he confessed to his spiritual advisors that he killed Grace Brown.

This New York State/Herkimer County historical marker, donated by the Farber family, is located outside the Herkimer County Jail. Today, jailhouse tours are regularly given by the Herkimer County Historical Society and highlight the cases of Chester Gillette ("An American Tragedy") and Roxalana "Roxana" Druse (the last woman hanged in the state of New York).

A historical marker, donated by the Farber family, currently rests outside the 1834 jail in Herkimer and reads: "In 1906, Chester Gillette was held here during his famous trial for the murder of Grace Brown, basis for novel 'An American Tragedy.'" Used as a model case for "circumstantial evidence," it has also been used as a subject for everything from folk songs to even ghost stories. However, the bulk of interest remains Theodore Dreiser's classic novel *An American Tragedy*, published in 1925.

A New Century

From 1900 to 1910, the population of Herkimer grew by over 33 percent to 7,420. While the publicity that surrounded the Gillette case certainly set the town on the map, it really wasn't needed. Nor was the flood that may have dampened the spirits and basements of many residents. Over the next decade the population would grow by more than 40 percent and reach an all-time high at 10,453. Business was booming throughout the valley and all the surrounding towns. A new Remington factory in Ilion began in 1914 to respond to the growing demand for firearms. In 1915, Remington began producing Enfield Pattern 14 rifles for a military contract with the British. And, other lucrative contracts followed. While the United States did its best not to enter World War I, it simply could not be avoided. The balance of power shifted in the Allies' favor when U.S. troops hit European soil in 1917.

A slight setback occurred in 1918, when an influenza pandemic outbreak killed more people in the United States than World War I. The devastating effects spread to Herkimer County. That same year, the Canal was enhanced by a larger waterway, the New York State Barge Canal. This new watercourse replaced much of the original route, leaving many abandoned sections (most notably between Syracuse and Rome).

So growing up in Herkimer County gave a youngster direct access to not only New York State history but the formation of our country—when you can see and even touch history, on a daily basis it becomes real. It's inspiring. And, there was more.

Herkimer County Courthouse is a three-story, wood frame structure with painted brick walls built in 1873. It features an octagonal tower with arched openings and a mansard roof. It was the site of the 1906 trial of Chester Gillette.

The geography of the area lent itself to natural resources beyond imagination and exciting developments in transportation. This attracted commerce, technology and innovation. Needs were met locally and nationally, by some of the country's finest manufacturers of goods and services. And, its greatest asset was the hard-working men and woman, who made their home, and raised their families amid the beauty of the Mohawk Valley.

Two

Luigi Giuseppe D'Ambrosio

"Time is the longest distance between two places."
—Tennessee Williams, *The Glass Menagerie*

It's impossible, right? To capture a person, without understanding the context of their life. Factors, other than an individual's origin, come into play. To understand these elements is to understand the subject. Along the journey of life, people forget how the road they took, not to mention the time they took it, shaped them as an individual. They underestimate the influence, be it consciously or unconsciously, of the environment and those they encountered. Often it takes the unfortunate loss of one of these elements to adequately place that impact into context.

Living in a country such as the United States, in a community such as Herkimer, New York, influences a person's life on a daily basis. It can enhance or detract an individual's goals. Thankfully, a person's soul keeps them anchored. Its strength drawn from faith, family and friendship. Positive forces that eclipse any negative influences.

As social beings we desire acceptance, some of which comes from our cultural environment. It is easier to bond with those who understand how we communicate, our behavior, and even how we worship. In addition to environmental influences, there is that of genetics.[1] The 20th century, in particular the second half, contributed greatly to the knowledge of genetic factors and their impact on human life. Ask any professional athlete: Which was of greater importance to their success, genetics or the environment, and you will realize how difficult it is to separate the two. Not to mention the importance of both.

The construction of the Erie Canal brought workers from around the globe including Italy. Italians worked side-by-side other immigrants, all with a common goal: prosperity. And when the waterway was complete many families stayed. Multiple generations assisted in sustaining the waterway. In 1896, while working in Syracuse, Italian workers employed by contractors McDonald & Sayre were making $1.20 a day improving the canal, and to the east, about 200 Italians were improving an aqueduct in Schenectady. They weren't always happy, but they worked hard for a fair wage; parenthetically, the group was also never hesitant to strike to have their needs met.

In 1900, 63,000 Italians came to America. This according to the Immigration Office at New York that also stated to the *Indianapolis Journal*: "Forty-seven thousand, of those that came last year were day laborers without a trade. About six thousand others were farmers, and they went to the agricultural districts of California, Louisiana and New Jersey. More than half of the whole number of Italian immigrants stay in New York State and the next largest number goes to Pennsylvania."[2]

Even those who returned to Italy eventually found their way back. And, when they did, they usually brought their family; incidentally, this typically meant they felt secure in the opportunities they found in America. According to some estimates 100,000 Italians were leaving Italy every year. As for upstate New York, the *Journal* stereotypically elaborated:

> There are 6,000 Italians in Utica, N.Y. The employed Italians of this city may be almost accurately apportioned to three occupations—fruit selling, tailoring and music. Nearly forty Italian tailors are employed in one of the big clothing factories of the city, and several of the merchant tailors employ Italians in their shops. Most of the remainder of the Italian men work in the fruit and vegetable commission houses in the neighborhood of Delaware and Maryland streets or peddle fruit from carts on the streets. The Italian musicians of the city are well known and popular among them the Montani family is most prominent.[3]

And, what was the cause of the heavy emigration from Italy? The *Journal* continued:

> Most of the Italians that leave Italy are from the southern part—Sicily, Calabria and the territory around Naples. That part is entirely devoted to farming or fishing and is less prosperous than the northern part of the country, which is actively commercial. The people in the south of Italy were held down to the ground a long time, kept in ignorance and heavily taxed. They became informed that this country was so rich that anyone could make a fortune in a short time and some of them rushed here.[4]

In 1907, the *Greenville Times* published another stereotypical view of the culture:

> The Italian is a genuine hustler. He comes over here for a job, takes whatever kind of work he can get, and sticks to it. I heard of a physician who served as a dishwasher, and a lawyer who worked for several years as a waiter until he could learn the language and become adjusted to the general scheme of things. One steamship line will have only Italian stevedores, because they work harder and are more temperate than the men of other nationalities. The enterprise and thrift of the Italians is indicated by the statistics, which show that in New York they have 4,000 real estate holdings values at $20,000,000. They own 10,000 stores in Manhattan and have $15,000,000 in the savings banks. There are two Italian steamship lines and sixteen daily and weekly papers.[5]

Taking a look at upstate New York, the *Times* noted: "In Utica, N.Y. the Italians have built themselves an opera house and provided a local stock company that gives very creditable performances to most courteous and enthusiastic audiences."[6]

While every culture seems to have their fair share of extraordinary athletes, some are quick to brag a bit louder than others. And, some are certainly justified. The Italian youth who loved boxing had plenty of outstanding pugilists to emulate. Those born prior to 1920 include:

> Salvatore Engotti, aka Sammy Angott (1915–1980); Mike Ballerino (1901–1965); Christopher "Bat" Batalino (1908–1977); Melio Bettina (1916–1996); Anthony "Tony" Canzoneri (1908–1959); Primo Carnera (1906–1967), Francesco Conte, Frankie Conley (1890–1952); Raffaele Giordano, aka Young Corbett III (1905–1993); Frankie Covelli (1913–2003); Samuel Lazzaro, aka Joe Dundee (1903–1982); Giuseppe Corrara, aka Johnny Dundee (1893–1965); Vincenzo Lazzara, aka Vince Dundee (1907–1949); Domenico Galento, aka Tony Galento (1910–1979); Frankie DiGennaro, aka Frankie Genaro (1901–1966); Angelo Geraci, aka Bushy Graham (1905–1982); Thomas Rocco Barbella, aka Rocky Graziano (1919–1990); Saverio Giannone, aka Joe Grim (1881–1939); Peter Gulotta, aka Pete Herman (1896–1973); Isadoro Jannazzo, aka Izzy Jannazzo (1915–1995); Ignacius Guiffi, aka Harry Jeffra (1914–1988); Rocco Tozzo, aka Rocky Kansas (1893–1954); Giuseppe DiMelfi, aka

Young Zulu Kid (1897–1971); Fidel LaBarba (1905–1981); Pete Latzo (1902–1968); Salvatore Mandala, aka Sammy Mandell (1904–1967); Anthony Marino, aka Tony Marino (1910–1937); Jay Nova, aka Lou Nova (1913–1991); Luigi Salica, aka Lou Salica (1912–2002); Peter Scalzo, aka Petey Scalzo (1917–1993); Mario Severino, aka Marty Servo (1919–1969); Giovanni Cervati, aka Little Jackie Sharkey (1897–1970); Phil Terranova (1919–2000); and Giocvanni Panica, aka Johnny Wilson (1893–1985).

Knowing what you are thinking, I'll say it for you, wow![7]

Ever since the days of the Erie Canal, it seemed that Italian and Irish immigrants often found themselves working side-by-side as a part of New York's booming economy; no doubt, the underlying commonality not only their community and employer, but often that of faith. While both cultures respected the Catholic Church, they also argued control and doctrine. It wasn't unusual for neighborhood enmity to overflow into schoolyards and even onto the streets. Ethnic lines could be drawn as fast as guns in the Wild West. And, thankfully it was fists that were fired rather than bullets.

The perceived Irish stronghold over boxing, thanks to names such as Sullivan and Corbett, altered the fight game. It forced some fighters, including Italian pugilists, into adopting nondescript monikers. Hey, if it meant feeding your family during tough economic times, then why not?

The Birth of a Champion

On Saturday, November 8, 1913, a severe storm crossed over the Great Lakes wreaking havoc with everything along its path. Two vessels ran aground, the *Louisiana* on Lake Michigan and the *Waldo* on Lake Superior. The storm, with its hurricane force wind, was headed toward upstate New York. However, it would not reach there until after the birth of Luigi Giuseppe D'Ambrosio. Luigi, or Lou, was the fifth child of Antonio and Louisa (Onorato) D'Ambrosio.

Antonio D'Ambrosio, born in Italy in 1870, arrived in New York in 1890.[8] His bride to be, Louisa, born in Italy in 1880, arrived in America in 1903. The pair married, and by 1905, welcomed the birth of their first child, Pasqualino. In addition to Antonio's family of three, they had a cousin and three borders living with them on Williams Street in Herkimer.[9] Antonio, age 35, and his cousin Banett Gallonio, age 19, were both woodworkers.[10] Their native language was spoken fluently in the home and on the streets of the Italian dominated section of Herkimer. Many of their neighbors, with surnames such as Gallo, Macri, Pistillo, and Strongo, to cite a few, all claimed Italy as their birthplace. And, solace could be found not only in speaking the same language but also in worship. Catholicism was at the heart of their existence and to have a service custom for their need was pivotal. When the growing Italian population of Herkimer expressed a desire for their own church, many of the residents stepped forward to assist, including Lou's father. St. Anthony's Society became the initial step toward that reality. The Rev. Thomas Cusack, Bishop of the Albany Diocese, heard the cry and approved establishing a church on September 25, 1916.

The Rev. Nicola Parrone was named the first rector of St. Anthony's Church and land was purchased for a place of worship on the west side of South Main Street. A cornerstone laying ceremony took place on June 16, 1917, and the new church was dedicated on September 1, 1917. (St. Anthony's Church exists to this day but no longer has the simple lantern and spire atop its modest construction.) The timing could not have been better: Pope Benedict XV was leading the Catholic Church and promulgating Canon Law. Also, in Fátima, Portugal, the story of a famous miracle began in May 1917, when three children, all under the age of ten, claimed to have encountered the Virgin Mary on their way home from tending a flock of sheep. This apparition was considered to be among the most important in the Catholic Church.

As the fifth child of a large and growing family, Luigi quickly understood the value of persistence. He also accepted that the likelihood of getting anything more than just secondhand clothing or toys was slim. It didn't bother him much because other things, such as stick ball, biking, hunting—be it for "Herkimer diamonds" or game—and fishing occupied most of his time. Similar to most kids, Luigi's imagination ran wild. He and his friends would dream about being characters from one of James Fenimore Cooper's novels, or reenact one of the local Revolutionary tales, while playing in the woods, or even scare one another while hastily strolling past the infamous 1834 jail on Main Street. They enjoyed translating the stories they heard at home, or in school, into their own form of reality. If competition yielded controversy, as it often did, Luigi was quick to take sides and even fight for what he believed in. Years later, he admitted being a tough guy, sort of a school bully. Unafraid to scrap if necessary, and occasionally without provocation, "Little Luigi" would stand his ground.

The D'Ambrosio children were educated at the South Side School located on South Main Street in Herkimer. The school, built in 1888, would see many a fine soul stroll through its hallways but none as beloved as Margaret E. Tuger. Greeted by about 200 students, in August 1891, she was delighted to learn most spoke English. However, commerce and immigration would soon increase her student population by five-fold and add multiple languages to her curriculum.

Consistency—for over half a century her classes opened every morning with the "The Lord's Prayer" and the singing of a patriotic song—was her strength and God and country her foundation. While there was no substitute for the basics, or the "Three Rs" as it was called: Reading, writing and arithmetic, there was also no replacement for respect. Ruling with an iron fist, and tools if necessary, she could also be as compassionate as a new mother. In retrospect, it was this behavioral polarity that may have been her biggest asset.

The Tuger family had moved to Baldwinsville, New York, in 1856. Tuger's German father, Adam, became a naturalized American citizen in 1862. And, when his country called him, he answered. He perished during the American Civil War (1861–1865), while two-months-old Margaret, born on November 10, 1864, was still in her crib.[11] Drawing on the strength of her widowed mother Eva, Tuger sought to become a teacher. At 16 that dream became a reality, but it took another decade before that vision was enhanced by her opportunity in Herkimer. Often admitting that she could have made a better salary elsewhere, she was also quick to point out that it would have been less satisfying. Tuger found the magic recipe in Herkimer, and she knew it.

Miss Tuger's arrival in Herkimer was as principal of the new South Side School. And soon, four teachers formed her staff. Insightful, as her foreign student base increased, Tuger modified her curriculum to include naturalization. She had an incomparable knack for empathizing with the need of others, undoubtedly a result of her own upbringing. Deeply religious, she made her daily prayer pilgrimage along South Main Street—often dressed in one of her tailored suits and trademark red hats—to St. Anthony's church. For her, as with so many others in the village, prayer was the perfect way to begin a day.

Walks between the school and her hotel (her home away from home) often took far more time than imagined. Constantly greeted by passersby, she insisted upon being courteous. Everyone knew her or knew of her. Luigi Giuseppe D'Ambrosio was one of "her boys." And, the youngster couldn't be prouder of it. This was despite being turned across her knee on occasion, when "Luigi," which she always called him, got out of line (everybody else always called him Lou, or Looey).

When the educational institution outgrew its walls, it was razed, and a new school was inaugurated in 1932. It was appropriately named: Margaret E. Tuger School.

The Roaring Twenties

By 1920, the D'Ambrosio family was living at their own home on Smith Street in Herkimer. With seven children, ranging in age from 2 to 15, space was at a premium. In addition to Pasqualino, there were Jennie, Filomenia, Biogio (Leslie), Lou, Angelo, and Joseph. Antonio, now a merchant, was a naturalized citizen and could speak broken English. Five years later, two other children had been added to the family: Anna, and Carmella. Antonio was employed as a Saloon Keeper, while Louisa tended the needs of the children.

On or about December 9, 1924, property occupied for a retail store and dwelling purposes, by Antonio D'Ambrosio and John Cognetto, was partially damaged and destroyed by an explosion and a fire. It was a two-story frame and brick building located at 109 West Smith Street, in the village of Herkimer. As a result of the tragedy, both D'Ambrosio and Cognetto had to engage in legal action to recover a portion of their loss. It wasn't a simple task and it added to the economic burden faced by Antonio.

For the D'Ambrosio family, similar to the many Italian households of the region, faith played a large role. It was the cornerstone of their existence. There are rites of passage in every religion and Catholicism was no different. Symbolic ceremonies, such as baptisms, Holy Communion, confirmation and confession would have a role in the lives of every member of the D'Ambrosio family. As a child, Lou, like most children, had a limited attention span. His mind wasn't on church, but that would soon change. In 1927, Father Gustave Purificato was named pastor of St. Anthony's church. He replaced Father Charles McCormack who had succeeded Father Parrone. Father Purificato realized that the long cold Herkimer winters could try the patience of a youth, unless as a matter of course you provided options. One of those alternatives was physical fitness that could include the sweet science.

Boxing was hugely popular in the United States, generating journalistic attention and crowds that often surpassed those of other athletic endeavors. It was especially prevalent among immigrant Catholics. After all, Gene Tunney, a devout Catholic, was heavyweight champion of the world in 1927. Father Purificato wasn't alone in his enthusiasm for the sport. Bishop Bernard Sheil, who founded the Catholic Youth Organization in Chicago, was another advocate.[12] He believed that pugilism promoted athletic and spiritual discipline. Since 1931, students at the University of Notre Dame raised money for missions in present-day Bangladesh through an annual series of boxing matches. Some historians, and even theologians, argue that there is a spiritual value on the experience of the body pain and thus boxing should be viewed in a different light.

Bishop Bernard Sheil, who founded the Catholic Youth Organization (CYO) in Chicago, was a boxing advocate. He believed that pugilism promoted athletic and spiritual discipline. *Library of Congress, LC-DIG-hec-34201 (digital file from original negative)*

Proper environmental conditions were required for children to grow into morally healthy adults and Father Purificato understood this; consequently, he suggested using the basement of the church for boxing instruction. The idea was a hit, as the youth parish flocked to the activity. Little did Lou know that he would recall for life the difficulty he had seeing punches thrown at him in that dimly lit basement. From those participating in the Catholic Bowling League to those punching a bag in the church basement, Father Purificato's charisma soon became apparent. He spoke to you and not at you, Ambers would often recall, and his demeanor was such that he exuded confidence to everyone he spoke to.

The Stock Market Crash of 1929 was a major stock market meltdown. It started on October 24 ("Black Thursday") and continued until October 29, 1929 ("Black Tuesday"), when share prices on the New York Stock Exchange collapsed. When taking into consideration the full extent and duration, it was nothing short of catastrophic. The United States crash, which followed the London Stock Exchange's crash of September, signaled the beginning of the 12-year Great Depression that affected all Western industrialized countries. It seemed as if nobody was spared. For example, in 1931 businesses nationwide were failing at a rate of more than 130 per day.

The massive joblessness of the 1930s struck home in Herkimer. Residents scrambled to make ends meet. Antonio, who owned a bar and confectionery store in town, lost it during the Depression. Most were forced to accept a no-frills lifestyle: Food was grown and preserved, transportation was on foot, clothes were made,

St. Anthony's Society evolved into St. Anthony's Church (pictured here), on South Main Street in Herkimer. Having outgrown its walls, a new St. Anthony's Church was dedicated across the street in 1964.

not purchased, and folks bartered for survival. Work was sporadic, but it puts food on the table and paid bills. Life was taken one day at a time.

In 1930, the D'Ambrosio family rented a home on Smith Street. Antonio was working odd jobs, while Louisa tended to the house, paying particular attention to the now three children under the age of ten: Anna, Carmella and the latest addition Thomas. Most of the family worked: Pasqualino often assisted his father, while Filomenia worked at a knitting mill. Both Biogio (Leslie) and

The cornerstone of St. Anthony's Church, commemorating its dedication on June 16, 1917, is shown here.

Luigi (Louis) were working at Standard Furniture Company, over on King Street in Herkimer, and young Joseph was a newsboy.[13] With such a dynamic family it was hard for Louisa to keep track of everyone, but she did her best.

It was at this time that, Luigi's interest in boxing grew exponentially. He began regular workouts in the basement of St. Anthony's Church, only a short walk from his home: To get to the church he walked two blocks west on Smith Street, then made a right on South Main. Crossing the street, he reached the front entrance of St. Anthony's after walking about 400 feet north. Encouraged by Father Purificato, along with many of his friends, his skills improved. And the youngster, albeit unassumingly, began pondering his next step. Recognizing his natural ability, Purificato would later compare his sprightly style to that of Harry Greb or Tony Canzoneri. To this day, it is difficult to imagine a parish leader so insightful and knowledgeable about pugilism.

Understanding that the only way he was going to improve as a boxer was to find better competition, Lou decided to step out of his comfort zone and test the water, so to speak. He made the difficult decision to participate in the many bootleg battles held in the region. Drawing solid talent, the weekly events attracted good crowds and paid well (initially, about two to four dollars). There was only one problem: his parents, particularly his mother, did not condone such activity. So, with the help of a few friends and family members, he executed a discreet plan. Taking the assumed name of Otis Paradise, a moniker believed constructed from a newspaper advertisement, Lou was off to places such as Schenectady, about 70 miles east as the crow flies, Glen Falls, about 100 miles northeast, and even to Kingston, about 125 miles south. Concerned about *all* of his family learning of the charade, he pledged everyone associated with the parody to secrecy.[14]

At first the bouts were relatively close to home. However as Lou's confidence grew, both in and out of the ring, the distance grew. And, as he believed, traveling a few extra miles could lead to better instruction, contacts within the fight game and earnings. Riding the rods or freighthopping, sleeping wherever he could, and seldom eating became a way of life. With no place to change his clothes and no clothes to change into, it could be a challenging existence. Estimates of Ambers' participation in bootleg battles, prior to 1932, range from a low of about dozen to almost five times that number.[15] Without records it's just too hard to obtain an accurate figure. (See Appendix A.)

A Product of Bootleg Boxing

Lou Ambers was a product of bootleg boxing—a term that stretches the definition of both amateur and professional. From about 1930 until the spring of 1933, the youngster catered to the needs of several promoters and was often compensated for his services. While promoters were licensed, many lacked sanctioning by the Amateur Athletic Union—few even followed State Commission regulations. At first the battles were fun, and a chance to hone his skills. But as the youngster improved, so did the level of competition he faced. Suffice it to say, enjoyment and experience quickly took a backseat to appropriate remuneration. In other words, Lou, similar to other participants, wanted to be paid what they were worth.

By 1932, matchmaker Dr. Carl J. "Doc" Studer, who was conducting the American Legion Monday night bouts in Kingston, New York, saw promise in Ambers, aka Brooklyn lightweight Otis Paradise.[16] Having utilized his services, he had witnessed the youngster's development and liked his style. Typically featuring two heavyweights—drawn from the many area clubs to participate in a six-round feature—Studer's promotions were extremely popular. But, if a lighter fighter, such as Paradise, became a popular attraction, he too could be considered for a main event. The cards also included a six-round semi-final, or even a special event, preceded by four 4-round preliminaries. A fighter's placement on the card determined his compensation.

Gaining a level of notoriety as a trainer, Studer worked with fight manager Walk Miller. He assisted in the development of the late pugilist "Tiger" Flowers, and only a few years before (1927), was resurrecting the career of Young Stribling. Studer also ran a gym in Kingston at Sahler's Sanitarium at 61 Wall Street. There he instructed in boxing, gymnastics and swimming. Studer's strength, as members of his fighting stable could attest, was confidence building.[17]

A fixture in Kingston boxing promotion from 1931 until 1933, Studer was suspended in 1934. (He resigned as Legion matchmaker in May and his license expired in November 1934.) The following year his interests shifted toward Poughkeepsie, New York.

Closer to home, Lou grabbed what opportunities he could. Legend had it that a Utica promoter who had often utilized the fighter's services, got fed up with his financial demands—Lou sought ten dollars instead of the usual seven for the better boxers—and decided to teach him a lesson. The impresario, former pugilist James "Red" Herring, contacted featherweight Frankie Wallace, aka Frankie Angelora, and asked the Cleveland resident if didn't mind picking up a quick "c-note," plus expenses, to put Paradise in his proper place. Herring, along with former minor league baseball player Art Mills, had been operating a gym in Utica, New York, since the late 1920s.[18] Like Studer, they too promoted "bootleg" boxing.[19] So, Frankie headed to Albany in the guise of a tutor. Entering the ring against Ambers, Wallace immediately tried to take control, only to be bombarded with punches that seemed to come from every direction. Upon learning that he had essentially defeated Frankie Wallace, the youngster's confidence hit the roof.[20]

The Year 1932

It was not a year for the faint of heart as unemployment in the U.S. reached 24 percent. Americans were living in the streets, under bridges or in abandoned vehicles. The population of Herkimer, New York, was also on a downswing. And, it began a trend that would not correct itself until the turn of the century.

Most boxing resources view the *legitimate* professional career of Lou Ambers beginning in June of 1932.[21] Fighting out of New York City haunts such as Fort Hamilton Arena, Englewood Arena, Lenox Sporting Club and New York Coliseum, Ambers sought and realized better wages and competition. Having already boxed under the surnames of both Ambers and Paradise, he continued to do so until spring 1933.

From June through August, Lou Ambers met and defeated Frankie Curry (also spelled Carey), Joe Pelicano (also spelled Pellicano) and Al Pieretti.

Curry (Carey) had been around since the twenties and was basically a club fighter. He held victories over Charlie Goodman and Abe Friedman.[22] A handful of fights from the end of his career, Curry, who substituted for Larry Ganley, was knocked out by Ambers at the 0:24 mark of the third round.[23] The June 9 contest was held at Fort Hamilton Arena.

Hailing from South Brooklyn, Joe Pellicano (Pelicano) had a pretty good career as a 118-pound amateur before turning pro in 1930. Fighting locally, he won a majority of his battles. Coming off a loss to Johnny Troncone, Pelicano hoped to redeem himself against Ambers on July 14. Instead, he took a six-round loss while receiving a solid beating. Unable to dance fast enough to avoid damage from his versatile opponent, Pelicano was simply a target. His nose was nearly broken in the second round, his right eye swelled in both the fourth and fifth, and he was dropped in the sixth. This contest was also held at the Fort Hamilton Arena.

Al Pieretti, from Lyndhurst, was an aggressive fighter who always started fast. Some believe he was a third-round knockout victim to Ambers on August 7. If so, the fight seemed to slip between the cracks due to poor record keeping.[24] It was in all probability a bootleg battle.

Beginning in September, Ambers, who was still discreetly battling as Otis Paradise, began bouncing back and forth between identities.

As Lou Ambers, he defeated New Jersey pug Mel Doty on September 6, at the Englewood Arena. It wasn't much of a challenge as Doty, a local warrior, was matched purely to park folks in the seats. There were times, as every good promoter understood, when popularity overshadowed talent.

Twenty days later, Ambers took on the tough lightweight by the name of Ray Meyers at the New Lenox Sporting Club in New York. The venue had an entertaining card of 36 rounds planned for that Monday night. With 35-plus battles under his belt, Meyers was the most experienced fighter Ambers would face all year. And, he looked forward to the task. Tipping at 127¾ pounds, Meyers was a standup type puncher with quick hands but little power. Ambers, who scaled at 132¾ pounds, took his adversary the five-round distance to win the feature event.

Next on the agenda was Phil Stark. As a tough and talented New York featherweight, his handlers were grooming him for bigger and better things. Stark, who turned pro in 1930, had only one recorded loss (Jerry Mazza). Ambers entered the November 14 battle at 131 pounds, or a pound up on Stark. The two fighters sparred to a six-round draw inside the New York Coliseum.

On to Carlstadt, New Jersey, on November 18, Lou Ambers tackled Jerry White at Zimmerman's Hall. White, who hailed from Jersey City, scaled at 134, while Ambers tipped two pounds lighter. White, who had boxed sporadically since 1928, lasted only four rounds before Ambers put him to sleep. Seemingly from nowhere, Ambers delivered a right hand to White's glass jaw and it was over.[25] The event, arranged by the Mayor's Relief Committee for the Unemployed, drew 1,000 fight fans.

From September through December, "Otis Paradise" battled, primarily if not exclusively, in Kingston, New York.

On September 12, Otis Paradise, who tipped at 133, engaged popular pug Johnny Marello, at 132, during a six-round semi-final held in Kingston, New York. The first two rounds appeared even. However, by the third term Marello, who hailed from Glasco, New York, began to tire. Paradise opened up a cut over Marello's eye in the fourth and that proved to be a game changer. While Marello did manage a few solid punches that stunned his adversary, after six rounds the fight belonged to Paradise.

Promising to be an exciting event, the American Legion benefit boxing show was being held at the outdoor venue on Broadway and West O' Reilly Street, on October 3. The evening's main event saw Eddie Sexton, the titleholder in the amateur Federation of Sports Clubs, draw Connecticut's own Phil Bronson in a slug fest. Substituting on an undercard for Johnny Marello, was Otis Paradise. Scaling a pound heavier than his opponent, he was more than happy to meet Buddy Emerson, the Saint Remy, New

York, lightweight. And, Marello, who was ironically in attendance, was more than happy to let him do so. To tell the truth, Johnny Marello wanted nothing to do with Buddy Emerson and his powerful right hand and felt Paradise, if he lived, would regret his decision. Marello even warned Paradise about what he was up against. Dancing appropriately around the punch, Paradise managed to successfully deliver enough left hands to close Emerson's left eye. At the end of the fifth round, when Emerson could no longer see, referee Bill Singer waved it off.[26]

A week later, it was once again American Legion boxing in Kingston as Otis Paradise tackled Nick Basso of Bristol, Connecticut, over six rounds. Back in August, the Glens Falls Amateur Sports Club conducted a show at the Halfway House outdoor arena. One of the participants of the event was Basso. In the audience were a number of Ambers' friends gathering intelligence. So, Otis Paradise was prepared for Basso's infighting style and relentless "elbowing." Overwhelmed by his antagonist, Basso did not last beyond the third round.[27]

Otis Paradise was clearly scheduled to meet Ralph Pignone of Poughkeepsie, New York, on Monday, November 14, at the Elks Club in Kingston. As a weaving, shifting and feinting fighter, Pignone was clever and uncommonly popular. However, Pito Perz substituted for Paradise and fought a six-round draw against Pignone.[28] Paradise, preferring to meet Phil Stark in the aforementioned contest, opted for a city paycheck instead.

Having yet to be defeated in a Kingston ring, Otis Paradise landed feature billing for the Elk's benefit boxing card on the November 21. His opponent was the capable boxer Benny Shields of Wingdale, near Poughkeepsie, New York. Appearing lethargic, Paradise struggled during the first round. Reprimanded by his corner, the youngster gathered his senses before leveling the Dutchess County mason twice to take the decision.

With the holidays just around the corner, the Elk's boxing card, on December 5, was conducted to fund Christmas baskets for the Kingston needy. In addition to the worthy cause, a bit of boxing entertainment was also provided. The main attraction of the evening was a dual between Otis Paradise, under the moniker Brooklyn Flash, and the ever so popular Tony White, of Pittsfield, Massachusetts. Impressing the smaller than anticipated crowd, with a variety of quick volleys, White's ego grew with every punch. Unimpressed, Paradise waited, then took command of the bout. Systematically using his left jab, Paradise rendered White helpless—he was simply unable to mount an attack. And, when White got a bit too confident by landing a combination, Paradise would send a powerful right hook to the body. A mistake by the card boy, or a blessing if you were Tony White, ended the battle a round short. In the end it was a five-round victory for Paradise.

Professional Boxing in 1932

Although there were times when Herkimer felt far removed from the rest of the world, it was never too far from a dream, or at least Lou Ambers thought so. Taking a look at the dynamic world of professional boxing in 1932: The heavyweights (unlimited weight) were ruled by Binghamton-born Jack Sharkey, with Max Schmeling and Max Baer contending; The light heavyweights (175 pounds) saw George Nichols as champion with Maxie Rosenbloom and Canadian Charlie Belanger breathing down his neck; French middleweight Marcel Thil ruled his class (160 pounds) with Vince Dundee and Gorilla Jones lurking in the shadows; Jackie Fields sat atop the welterweight (147 pounds) division with Lou Brouillard and Young Corbett right behind; the featherweights (126 pounds) had Buffalo-born Gaetano Alfonso Papa, aka Tommy Paul, sitting on the division thrown. The Papa brothers, which also included Bartolomeo "Al," Michele "Mickey," and Vito Antonio "Tony Jr.," followed their brother Tommy into the ring. He had Englishman Nel Tarleton and a few others watching him closely; the bantamweights (118 pounds) were looking up to Al Brown, while Newsboy Brown and Kid Francis were lurking about.

In the mid–1930s, photojournalist Alan Fisher documented the struggles of The Great Depression. Using Lou Ambers as a model, as it would later prove, was an excellent choice. In an all too familiar scenario, Otis Paradise, aka Lou Ambers, hops a freight car. *Library of Congress, LC-USZ62-128436 (b&w film copy negative)*

In 1932, Lou Ambers, aka Otis Paradise, was fighting for the experience and a paycheck. Any dreams he had about being a lightweight contender, were just that. That class was ruled, I mean *ruled*, by Tony Canzoneri. Watching his every move was Billy Petrolle, Sammy Fuller, Tracy Cox, Barney Ross, Jack Portney, Wesley Ramey, Tony Herrera, Cecil Payne, and Lew Massey. Sitting above the lights, in the junior welterweight (140 pounds) class were Johnny Jadick, along with Billy Petrolle (participation in multiple weight classes was common), and Jackie Kid Berg. Below the lights, at the junior lightweight (130 pounds) class you had Kid Chocolate, along with Benny Bass and Al Foreman. (The last two classes were not recognized by all associations. Hey, it's boxing!)

THREE

1933—You're Getting to Be a Habit

"Success is a science; if you have the conditions,
you get the result."—Oscar Wilde

In 1933, it became clear that Luigi Giuseppe D'Ambrosio was making a habit out of winning in the ring.[1] He was defining himself, creating his own successful style, both as Otis Paradise and as Lou Ambers.[2] And, it was a good thing, as 1933 proved to be the worst year of the Depression—unemployment peaked at just over 25 percent.

The world was undergoing change as Adolf Hitler became the chancellor of Germany (1933–1945) and established the totalitarian Third Reich. Few realized, although some had foreseen his intent, that his expansionist foreign policy would precipitate World War II, while his fanatical anti–Semitism would lead to the Holocaust.

Striking at the Heart

The happy-go-lucky days of the Roaring Twenties had clearly come to a conclusion by 1933. The economic collapse that had struck first in the large cities, had planted itself firmly in the small towns. Everyone, or so it appeared, was struggling with some aspect of their life. The D'Ambrosio family could certainly attest to the economic challenges in the Village of Herkimer. As Lou and his siblings walked the streets, the changes were evident. At the height of the Depression, residents were shocked by the businesses that were closed. Those that somehow remained open, did so often on a week-by-week, or day-by-day basis. Taking a closer look:

Open on Albany Street: Automobile dealer Munger & Bechtold; W.E. Day, Warren W. Conly and Pringle's Service Station were still fixing automobiles; C.R. Snell & Sons were meeting lumber needs, and G.A. Vielhauer was operating Carlton Restaurant.

On Main Street, or the heart of the village: car dealer Robert Johnston was doing his best to keep Baker & Fagan Motors running; Lanning & Folts, also a car dealer remained open; George Out's In & Out cigars and tobacco shop was still welcoming their customers; P.J. Dinneen and Myers Clothing Store remained open; Gerwig-Laird Coal Company and L. Schermer were still supplying customers; Baxter's Confectionery, also with a shop over in Ilion, remained open; Grocer L. Ernest Scott was still offering a helping hand; Hotel Waverly continued to greet guests; Kirby Office Equipment Company was supplying their customers; Acme Paper Box Company was welcoming business; A.A. McCoy still had the restaurant open, and Abram Zoller, County Surrogate Judge, was still holding court.

Turning down Mohawk Street, of those noteworthy businesses still open: Herkimer Body Works; Tucker's Tire Service & Veetyde Service Station, and Herkimer Gas & Oil, under Fred Brown, was still busy. Open over on Park Avenue; M.S. Harter was tending to electrical needs, as Brayton Flowers still added a touch of color to everyone's day.

Looking at Prospect: Smith Brothers' Garage was open; Prospect Hotel & Coffee Shop, was still serving a hot cup, and Nagle Sheet Metal Works was operating. Open on Washington Street: Herkimer New & Used Auto Parts under the watchful eye of Philip Rosenfeld, and Thomas Donlon, the glove manufacturer always looked busy.

With the average laborer's wage at $20 per week, boxing, as Ambers saw it, was a viable alternative. While the repeal of prohibition in the United States eased the pain of some, it was only temporary.

The Year 1933

In what would be a prolific year of boxing, Luigi D'Ambrosio would split his time between boxing identities. Although he managed to keep the Otis Paradise charade going until the end of April 1933, by that point his style and ring proficiency were too difficult to mask. Some of the beat writers had even picked up on the dual identities, so it was only a matter of time before the word went public. The local battles, not recognized by all sources, were likely bootleg contests.

Otis Paradise failed to appear for his first contest of the year in Kingston, on January 6. The six-round clash was against Joe "Marty" Moskovitz. It was the Mayor's Benefit Show for the Unemployed and matchmaker Studer had inked Paradise to the feature event. The impresario had gone on record stating Moskovitz would beat Paradise—whether or not this played into the fighter's decision not to attend was unclear.[3] Davey Jones, who substituted for Paradise, lasted a mere 50 seconds into the second round before Moskovitz put him to the canvas.

In between both Moskovitz events, above and below, Paradise may have taken a six-round loss to Lou Browne in Kingston.[4] While debatable, it certainly was feasible. For the past six months Browne had been living in Poughkeepsie to increase his exposure to the city (Manhattan and Brooklyn) fight game.

On January 30, the advertisement, on page 10 inside the *Kingston Daily Freeman*, proclaimed that Joe "Marty" Moskovitz was tackling Otis Paradise inside the old armory at 8:30. Also, six other bouts were also part of the evening's entertainment. General admission was 50 cents, chair seats were one dollar and reserved seating was a dollar and a half. Unfortunately for Moskovitz, that was as far as the tackling went as Paradise danced around him as if he was stuck in cement. Paradise controlled the action with his left jabs and when he saw a shot, as he did in the fourth term, he took it. A sharp right uppercut sent Moskovitz to the canvas for a count of four before being saved by the bell. Frustrated, Moskovitz fouled his antagonist in the sixth and final term. At that point, it was his only option to an aggressive assault.

It was back to the old armory in Kingston on April 11, as Otis Paradise defeated Babe Lancaster in a five-round technical knockout. Paradise just pummeled Lancaster's left eye with a right cross until it swelled to the size of a peach and forced a stoppage by Referee Bill Singer. Lancaster's clowning style initially caught Paradise off guard; consequently, a few solid left hooks to the body nearly floored the fighter. The battle, which was likewise

A rare broadside used to promote the fight between Joe Moskovitz and Otis Paradise, aka Lou Ambers. The bootleg battle was held on January 30, 1933, in Kingston, New York.

the main event, attracted about 500 fans. Benefiting from the card was the American Legion Welfare Fund, and naturally Studer. In all probability, not a single person in attendance ever thought it was the last ring appearance of Otis Paradise. As for Ambers, no tears were shed, as the masquerade had served its purpose.

Lou Ambers' fight year began in New York City. Still bouncing between identities, he had a number of fights in the queue. Outpointing Pedro Nieves over five lackluster rounds at the Coliseum, on February 22, would be the first. A Puerto Rican fighter living in New York, Nieves was less than a dozen fights into his professional career. However, he was coming off an impressive win over Al Casimini, three weeks ago at St. Nicholas Arena. As was the case with many of the routine boxing matches being held in or around the city, the result was incorrectly reported by a couple of newspapers.[5]

Tomato can Paul Scalfaro, who hailed from the Bronx, was simply a punching bag for Ambers on March 20. Outpointed over five rounds at the Jamaica Arena, Scalfaro was just picking up a paycheck.[6] Ambers would return to the venue two weeks later.

Charley Badami wasn't a knockout puncher, but a crafty fighter who knew how to win—eight consecutive victories, leading into his duel with Ambers, were proof. "The Mohawk Terror," just the first of a handful of monikers the fighter would earn along his fistic journey, delivered six solid rounds against Charley Badami but came up empty. Fans at Jamaica Arena saw a close fight on April 3, but in the end the verdict was a draw. Starting out strong, Ambers staggered Badami with a right cross in the very first round. It shocked some who had never seen Badami so susceptible so early in a contest. Fighting somewhat even in the second and third frames, both boxers appeared far more defensive. On target all evening, Ambers effectively countered Badami's slapping assaults. But his antagonist's persistence was enough to prohibit Ambers from mounting a successful offensive. Mirroring the ring hostilities was the damage assessment: The Herkimer pugilist suffered only a small cut under his left eye, while a nose-bleeding Badami had difficulty seeing out of his right optic.

Scheduled to rematch with Charley Badami on April 10, in New York, Ambers opted instead to head back to central New York. As mentioned, Paradise met Babe Lancaster the following day in Kingston.

Following a couple of local confrontations, Lou Ambers headed back to New York City in May. With well over a dozen fights in the months ahead, he was going to be busy. For a short period of time, Lou's sister, Philomena, joined her brother, as the pair rented a Bronx apartment. Managing their everyday living obligations, along with the finances, helped tremendously. And, she always remembered to send a portion of her brother's ring earnings home to their family in Herkimer.

Inside the Jamaica Arena, on May 22, Ambers, who tipped at 134½ pounds, stopped seasoned Cuban feather Tommy Barredo at the 2:23 mark of the second session. Wast-

ing little time, the Herkimer pugilist parked a stiff right square in the face of Barredo. Appearing out on his feet, the Cuban tumbled toward the ropes. Flailing about, Barredo tried to regain his footing but could not. It was then that Referee Jack Britton—yes, the former welterweight champion himself—stopped the contest. The action surprised few, as Ambers dropped his antagonist for a count of four in the opening round. Barredo, was one fight removed from the end of his ring career. Having lost his previous six duels, he was no match for Ambers.[7]

Scheduled to meet Ernie Tedesco over in Englewood, New Jersey, on June 26, Ambers was disappointed when the fight failed to materialize. Not just because he wanted to meet Tedesco, but he had bills to pay. The following day, Ambers substituted for veteran Joey Kaufman who was appearing on the Pete

World welterweight boxing champion William J. Breslin, aka Jack Britton, was born in Clinton, New York. His brilliant boxing career, begun in 1904, spanned a quarter century.
Library of Congress, LC-DIG-ggbain-11706 (digital file from original negative)

DeGrasse versus Petey Hayes fight card. Nothing short of a great opportunity, Ambers took a six-round victory over Tony Scarpati at the Fugazy Bowl in Brooklyn. A familiar fixture in New York amateur boxing, Scarpati had won the *Daily News* Golden Gloves' open championship at featherweight in 1931. He was struggling of late, as his management attempted to work him up in competition. Scarpati, just over twenty bouts into his career, could trade punches with some of the best of his class—if they stood still. However, a quick combination fighter such as Ambers could dance around him like a hummingbird over a sunflower.

The Fugazy Bowl, as most fight fans knew, was a stadium on Coney Island in Brooklyn. Originally called the Coney Island Stadium, it was renamed after one of its popular promoters, Humbert Fugazy. Situated on Surf Avenue near West Sixth Street, it saw its fair share of talented fighters including: Lou Salica, Mike Belloise, Ruby Goldstein, Midget Wolgast, Bob Olin, to name some. The venue could hold up to 12,000 people. Many fight fans became familiar with the venue thanks to Jack Dempsey's short-lived involvement.

Watching Ambers perform from ringside was a short, stout gentleman, who if you had to guess his occupation by his confident countenance, was maybe a tailor. He was not. The aura of rubbing alcohol, sweat, and hot pastrami gave it away. His name was Al Weill, and he was a boxing manager. Wearing metal-rimmed glasses that he pushed up by twitching his nose, he appeared overly energetic. You know, similar to a pacing expectant father in a hospital waiting room. Impressed by what he saw, Weill forsook the idea of observing the main event in favor of a trip to the dressing room of Lou Ambers. Following a brief introduction, the boxing manager extended an invitation. Afraid Lou would notice the dollar signs in his pupils, Weill invited Ambers & Company to his office the following day.

So, accompanied by his long-time friend and trainer, Frank "Skid" Enright, Lou Ambers journeyed to Weill's headquarters the next morning. Wasting little time, Weill got straight to the point: Ambers was as good a fighter as he could be without being a hell of a fighter. All he was lacking was Weill's management. Politely listening, Ambers nodded his head in affirmation: Obviously he wanted to be a champion. If Weill could get him there, Ambers was interested. However, his terms included having Enright in his corner, or no deal. Weill balked a bit, twitched his glasses up his nose a few times, then agreed. No contracts were signed, as Ambers' word was his bond.

Al Weill

Dubbed "The Vest" or "The Weskit" by journalist Dan Parker, Weill was seldom seen without a sleeveless, close-fitting waist-length garment worn over his shirt. At first glance, the look may have appeared unnatural on the fireplug, but looks can be deceptive. Weill could give Fred Astaire a run for his money on the dance floor, and that's no joke.

Armand Weill was born in Gebweiler, Alsace-Lorraine, France, on December 28, 1893. Upon coming to this country at the age of 10, he lived with relatives in Yorkville, part of the Upper East Side of Manhattan.[8] Taking a fancy to the sweet science, Weill managed to snag a job as a porter for John "The Barber" Reisler, one of the era's premier fight managers. Known on Broadway for many years as a barber, wheeler-dealer, club manager, fight manager, con man, and friend of anybody who thought they were somebody,

Reisler's claim to fame was becoming one of Jack Dempsey's first managers, then suing him for breach of contract—thankfully, Doc Kearns, on behalf of Dempsey, paid John the Barber off.

Brushing against Reisler, eventually landed Weill a job as a second. Since Reisler had a decent, yet fluctuating stable, it was good experience. And, the dough wasn't bad either. But it wasn't long before the second realized he'd rather be first, so he became a fight manager. He took a pug named Andy Brown on as client. That was before Brown went off to war and left Weill high and dry. With few alternatives, Weill turned his back to pugilism and put on a new pair of shoes. Yep, the boxing manager turned ballroom dancer could cut a rug as good as he could cut a fight contract. Since the dance halls were flourishing before World War I, Weill was in his element. He even dominated the Yorkville dance halls with his proficient waltzing.

When the pugs returned home from World War I (1918), and the Walker Law went into effect (1920), Weill was ready to reenter the ropes. Not only did he have the second license ever issued after the law went into effect, but one of the fighters in his stable won the first decision under the legislation. Speaking of fighters, Weill maintained a stable of just under a dozen and always managed to keep them occupied. And, he was also busy as a matchmaker—at one point running shows at three venues.[9]

Connecticut was one state that thrived under Weill's promotions. He produced shows at the New Haven Arena, White City Arena in West Haven, and the old amphitheater on Wethersfield Avenue in Hartford. Of some of the name fighters that dropped by "The Nutmeg State": Tony Canzoneri, Kid Chocolate, Sixto Escobar, Tommy Farr, Johnny Dundee, Al Gainer, and Eddie Reed.

Ironically, a relationship Weill managed to retain was with Jack Dempsey. In their younger days, the pair roomed together while trying to make ends meet.

Weill encountered Ambers when he was scouting talent for businessman Tim Mara. It was by accident that he happened into the Herkimer pugilist, then an unknown, battling against Tony Scarpati. Love at first fight, Weill put the press on Ambers to consider coming under his management—which he agreed to, following the conclusion of his current contract.

A seasoned boxer from Newark, New Jersey, Ernie Tedesco was simply disassembled by Lou Ambers. It happened on July 3, at the Englewood Sportsmen's Club. Before 300 fans, Ambers, who scaled at 132, systematically inflicted damage to the countenance of Tedesco, who tipped two pounds heavier. Exhausted from his initial offensive, Ambers came out slower in the sixth and final round. As he continued the onslaught, the Newark boxer could do nothing more than roll with the punches. As the last few seconds ticked off, Tedesco, covered with sweat and blood dripping down his face, just stood against the ropes. Gloves to his side, he was completely helpless. To cries of "finish him off," Ambers paused as if receiving a telegraph message one word at a time, then looked into the eyes of Tedesco. He refused to hit his antagonist. There were times in the ring, where enough was enough, and this was one of those times. The action spoke volumes regarding the character of the fighter.

Privately, he was criticized for his lack of killer instinct. Even so, Ambers never wished harm to an opponent, only to defeat them. He was competitive by nature, but not to the extent that it would violate his beliefs. And, he was precisely that, a man of religious conviction.

It was a charity event, for the Brooklyn Free Milk Fund for Children, and it was to be held at the Fugazy Bowl on July 11. The main event featured Midget Wolgast, NBA world's flyweight champion battling popular East Side fighter Lew Farber. Matched for six rounds against the popular Brownsville boxer Lou Feldman, Ambers was primed for the contest. However, the fight was delayed and rescheduled for July 13. Instead of meeting Feldman on that date, the "Terror of the Mohawk," who weighed 133, met his substitute, Harlem lightweight Patsy LaRocco, who hit 129¾. And, the Herkimer warrior simply destroyed LaRocco to capture the unanimous six-round verdict. Far too fast and clever for his opponent, Ambers dropped his adversary in the second round and had him nearly out in the third. For the record: Farber defeated Wolgast.

A mere 38 seconds into the third round, Al Pieretti hit the canvas from a crippling punch delivered by Lou Ambers. And, it wasn't a surprise to anyone who had witnessed the Herkimer fighter simply dominating his opponent during the previous rounds. The event, held on July 17 at Englewood, New Jersey, was the largest crowd of the season. Razor sharp, Ambers delivered snappy combinations and overhand rights at will. A seasoned fighter who debuted in 1928, Pieretti, who hailed from Newark, hadn't won a fight an over a year.[10]

It was off to West Springfield, Massachusetts, on July 31, as Lou Ambers was slated to meet Roland LeCuyer. A native of Holyoke, Massachusetts, LeCuyer was a streaky featherweight who debuted back in 1927. Scheduled for eight rounds, Ambers needed only three before sending his antagonist to dreamland. Maintaining a demanding pace, the Herkimer fighter was compiling victories faster than rifles coming off the Remington assembly line back in Ilion.

Appearing at the Polo Grounds, or the largest venue he had ever fought at, Lou Ambers found it hard to curtail his excitement. And, understandably so, as this was the venue where only a decade ago, heavyweight champion Jack Dempsey fought Luis Firpo. Holding over 50,000 fans, it was a vision to behold. On a night that saw middleweight Ben Jeby become the eleventh boxing champion to relinquish his title (to Lou Brouillard) so far this year, Lou Ambers was part of an impressive undercard. It was the evening of August 9, and Ambers, aka "Terror of the Mohawk," tackled Jack Rose, one of Hymie Caplan's protégés.[11] (By the way, Jeby was also managed by Caplan, hence the match.) Having fought well until this year, Rose held recent victories over Al Casimini and Benny Whitier. Scaled at 133, or two pounds heavier than his opponent, Ambers moved about the ring with such style that he easily captured the six-round decision. While Rose had more power to his punches, he simply could not snare Ambers.

The Polo Grounds was also home to the New York Giants. The baseball club, in the franchise's fifty-first season, was on their way not only to winning the National League pennant, but beating the Washington Senators, of the American League, in the 1933 World Series. Although he wouldn't admit it, Ambers got a kick out of walking through the same hallways frequented by Carl Hubbell, Hal Schumacher, Travis Jackson, Mel Ott and Bill Terry.

On August 14, over in Springfield, Massachusetts, Lou Ambers outpointed Joe Ferrante, aka Honey Mellody, over ten rounds. Mellody, who substituted for Johnny Gaito, hailed from Boston, and was far from a knockout artist. However, he held victories over Vernon Cormier and Al Gauthier. The fighter was often confused with William (Honey) Mellody, a gifted fighter from an earlier era.

Charley Badami, who scaled at 136, drew Lou Ambers, who tipped a pound lighter, over six rounds at the Fugazy Bowl in Brooklyn on August 29. As you recall, the pair last

The Polo Grounds, located in Upper Manhattan, New York City, was used for numerous sporting events including boxing. In 1933, Lou Ambers fought twice inside the prestigious venue.
Library of Congress, LC-DIG-ggbain-13792 (digital file from original negative)

met back on April 9 in the Jamaica arena and fought to the identical result. This was the rescheduled rematch. Badami scored with his calling card, or overwhelming left hooks to the body. Thankfully, Ambers was swift enough to avoid some. When he could, he countered, and thankfully it was enough to keep him in the fight. The fans enjoyed it and it looked as if the pair had developed quite a rivalry.[12]

When Tony Canzoneri won his first championship, the World Featherweight title, with a 15-round decision over Benny Bass on February 10, 1928, he captured the hearts of many Italian Americans including Luigi D'Ambrosio—to say that the youngster was in awe of Canzoneri would certainly be an accurate assessment. When Ambers learned he had been placed on the undercard of the championship fight between Barney Ross and Tony Canzoneri, on September 12, he just couldn't believe it.

When Lou Ambers closed his eyes at night, and dreamed of being a professional boxer, Tony Canzoneri was that man. Back on November 20, 1931, Ambers' adoration led him to stealing a ride on a freight train in order to attend Canzoneri's title defense against Kid Chocolate at Madison Square Garden. Boarding an iron horse out of Herkimer, at six o'clock in the morning, with just short of $3.00 in his pocket, Ambers arrived around four o'clock in the afternoon. Unsure if he could make it to the fight, yet alone return to Herkimer after the event, the youngster checked into the Y.M.C.A.—he needed a place to lay his head afterwards. At the Garden, the best seat he could afford was in the gallery. As he stared at Canzoneri dancing between the ropes, he pictured himself in the identical spot. That was where he wanted to be.

Scheduled to meet the New Jersey Lightweight champion Joey Costa on September 12, Ambers understood it wasn't going to be at the Garden, but it wasn't a bad venue either. He was back inside the Polo Grounds. Although his title was new, Costa, who debuted in 1927, had been around the fight game for years. By the time the Jersey City pugilist reached Ambers, he held victories over Tommy Crowley, Lew Feldman, Johnny Lucas, and Charlie Van Reedon. Both fighters were just thrilled to be on the championship undercard.

Lou Ambers, who tipped the scales at 134½, captured the six-round semi-final by outpointing Joey Costa, who scaled two pounds lighter. Honestly, few thought Costa had the speed to catch his elusive opponent. And, they were right. Ambers delivered a sound performance until he injured his thumb. After the battle, instead of gushing over the injured first digit of his hand, he hustled out of the dressing room to catch the main event. With great care he observed the moves of Canzoneri, flinched when he lost three rounds to low blows and hoped in his heart that the fighter could grab the split decision. However, such was not the case as Barney Ross had taken enough rounds to be victorious.[13] The result didn't dampen an evening that Ambers saw as a wish granted.

Damon Runyon

> "*Always try to rub against money, for if you rub against money long enough, some of it may rub off on you.*"—Damon Runyon, *A Very Honorable Guy*

Using words, but no brush, Damon Runyon painted the 1930s perfectly for the time. His vernacular portraits of the Broadway gambling scene grew out of the prohibition era and captivated readers. And, if you wanted to be somebody you rubbed against Runyon. That was because anybody who was anybody was likely to end up included in his newspaper column. In September, the famed author, short-story writer and newspaperman, mentioned Lou Amber (missing the "s") in his syndicated column titled "Great Crops of Juvenile Fighters Ranging From 124 to 130 Pounds Are Residing in New York Area." Why not a plug for the local boys? On the list of names given, Runyon only singled out a few: Mike Belloise, Benny Britt and Lou Amber, of Herkimer, New York. The incident was like having your name placed on a marquee. Seemingly overnight, Ambers became a celebrity.

People, especially individuals such as Ambers, aka Otis Paradise, fascinated Runyon. Aware of the boxer's dual identities the wordsmith got a kick out of the deception. He even believed Paradise mimicked some of the qualities of his characters.[14]

A "Damon Runyon character" evoked a distinctive social type and New Yorkers loved the rub. The writer even contributed an adjective to the English language: Runyonesque. The word defined as relating to, or characteristic of, Damon Runyon or his style, language, or imagery. The writer's often colorful and entertaining stories involved actors, gamblers, gangsters, hustlers and shysters. Colorful monikers, such as "Sky Masterson," "Nathan Detroit," and "Harry the Horse," quickly became his trademark. One need only to refer to *Guys and Dolls*, perhaps his best-selling book, to get a flavor of Runyon. Published only the previous year (1932), Runyon's fire was lit and there was no putting it out.

Ambers took a big chance on September 25, when he entered a ring against hometown favorite Stanley Krannenberg (aka Stanley Kranberg) in Englewood, New Jersey.[15] His thumb still bothered him, even though the fight was postponed a week to allow him more time to heal. Knowing that his tall opponent was a defensive fighter without a knockout punch, no doubt supported his confidence. Ambers, who scaled at 133, captured the eight-round decision over Krannenberg, who tipped at 136½. Coming out in the first, he bounced around the ring like a pinball—the action seemed to baffle his opponent, who frankly had no idea what to do. So, Krannenberg tried to clinch and dampen the actions of his antagonist, but it accomplished little. Managing to cut Ambers' eye in the second frame, that too failed to impact the "Herkimer Terror." Ambers easily took all subsequent rounds while also drawing blood from his antagonist's muzzle.

The fight was delayed for twenty minutes due to a bizarre event. Englewood promoter Ralph Yandola, whose behavior had been erratic all season long, was panic stricken. Robbed of $200 by the club's secretary, he was lost for words and cash. Thus, none of the participants were assured of payment for their services. The impatient crowd of 750 fans had no idea what was happening. Yandola did his best to pacify the boxers with promissory notes, however most of the boxers left with no idea when, or even if, they would ever be paid. On a positive note, the thumb of Ambers appeared healed.

Originally from Grand Rapids, Michigan, Stanley Krannenberg, who had been successful in the Midwest, decided to head west in January (1933). He was ready for the next level, or so he believed. Failing miserably, first in California and the Washington—in nine

Another photograph of Lou Ambers, used as a model for photojournalist Alan Fisher, portraying a struggling survivor of the Great Depression. *Library of Congress, LC-USZ62-128434 (b&w film copy negative)*

ring battles he won only one bout—he returned to New Jersey. The storyline was all too common in the fight game. In a career that would end in December, Krannenberg always claimed Lou Ambers was the finest fighter he ever faced.

For his next three autumn battles, Lou Ambers headed east to the Valley Arena in Holyoke, Massachusetts—a stronghold for New England pugilism. First, Ambers outpointed Johnny Gaito over ten lackluster rounds on October 9. Gaito, who hailed from Yonkers, was a talented fighter who was on the tail end of a solid career. He held victories over Johnny Harko, Sid Terris and Johnny Scalzi. Even so, he was a working for a paycheck, and it showed.

On October 23, Ambers captured a ten-round decision over New York fighter Phil Rafferty. Having fought since 1929, Rafferty had recently become familiar to New York opponents as a distance punching bag. That said, he was making money doing it: He was at the losing end of a decision victory against Benny Leonard last year, and even took a split-decision victory over Battling Battalino in August. Rafferty fought as anticipated: He stayed out of range and trouble to last the distance.

In a far better performance, Lou Ambers simply dominated veteran Providence pugilist Paris Apice, over ten rounds, to take a unanimous decision on October 30.[16] As Apice was coming off two solid victories, the first against Henry Emond, and the second against Frankie Carlton, the partisan Holyoke crowd expected a bit more from the New England boxer. Ambers, aware that Apice won the 1928 Rhode Island and New England Amateur Flyweight titles, was pleased with the result. He hoped to avoid his antagonist's crippling combinations and did just that. He was on his game: accurate, powerful and in control.

Stanley Winneryk, who weighed 132, met Lou Ambers, two pounds heavier, at the Arena in Philadelphia on November 27. Winneryk, who hailed from Lawrence, Massachusetts, was at the end of a good career that saw him victorious over some good boxers including Pete DeGrasse, Jerry LaMontagne, and Joe Foglietta. If this was going to be the end of the line, or so he believed, he wanted to make it memorable. And, it was, but not for the reasons he had hoped. In the second round, Ambers blasted a right hand to the jaw that landed with such force that it sounded as if a tree snapped. It struck Winneryk so hard that it lifted him off his feet. Landing under the ropes, he instinctively popped up before the count began. However, unable to identify the planet he was on, the referee waved it off. The Monday night crowd, not to mention matchmaker Pete Tyrrell stood in awe over the power exhibited by Ambers.[17] The fight was a preliminary to the main event that featured Eddie Cool versus Frankie Klick. If you had to pick a point in Ambers' career where it became obvious that he was more than a preliminary fighter, it was this night at the Philadelphia Arena; furthermore, *Philadelphia Inquirer* clearly supported the claim in their column "The Old Sport's Musings."

On December 5, it was off to the Rhode Island Auditorium in Providence to meet Herbert Lewis Hardwick, aka Cocoa Kid. Honestly, Ambers was a bit surprised at the lack of opposition displayed by the New Haven boxer. Having dropped the Puerto Rican born pugilist three times, Ambers sailed to a decision victory.

For Christmas, Ambers, who scaled a bulky 145 (reports vary), wrapped up (outpointed) "Young" Joe Firpo, who tipped five pounds lighter, and sent him home to Penn's Grove. A seasoned veteran, Firpo debuted back in 1926—he had over 100 career fights.[18] Eight one-sided rounds saw Lou Ambers victorious in the Arena semi-final. The Philadelphia feature bout saw Frankie Klick deliver the flashy Cuban "bon bon" (Kid Chocolate) in the seventh round via a stunning right.

As the year drew to a close, Ambers reflected on what had taken place. Was he satisfied? Yes, about as satisfied as a fighter in his shoes could be at this stage of his career. Was he excited? Yes, without question.

He bid farewell to his alter ego, Otis Paradise, a fighter, who by his own admission, contributed to his amateur/bootleg fight total of 136. Incidentally, and worth reminding everyone, the total fluctuated with the passing of time. The charade had served its purpose and the cat was clearly out of the bag. Blame it on Damon Runyon—although others knew of his dual identities—if you prefer, but don't hold it against the brilliant writer who also penned Amber(s) into one of his columns. The action catapulted the boxer into the forefront of promising pugilists, or so it appeared.

COCOA KID

Born: May 2, 1914
Mayaguez, Puerto Rico

Died: December 27, 1966
Chicago, Illinois

Bouts: 244
Won: 176
Lost: 56
Drew: 10
KOs: 48

Real Name: Herbert Lewis Hardwick

Monikers: Louis Kid Cocoa

Weight Class: Welterweight
                   Middleweight

Height: 5 ft 10 in   Reach: 68.5 in

Herbert Lewis Hardwick, aka Cocoa Kid, was inducted into the International Boxing Hall of Fame, in Canastota, New York, in 2012. Possessing a punishing left jab, along with a destructive right cross, the boxer participated in the fight game for nearly two decades.

And, the Herkimer fighter couldn't ask for more: For five weeks Ambers was a sparring partner for his mentor, Tony Canzoneri. And, he even appeared on one of his undercards. One wonders just how many times Ambers pinched himself to prove he wasn't hallucinating

In early summer, Ambers caught the attention of boxing manager Al Weill. As Tim Mara's matchmaker, Weill was assisting in a return match between Canzoneri and Ross. Mara was perhaps best known for his co-promotion, along with Jack Dempsey, of the heavyweight title between Max Baer and Max Schmeling. Only three years ago, Weill had teamed with Dick Gray, to drop anchor in New London, Connecticut. There they established the Thames Arena, where Weill began making and promoting matches. Although Ambers was still a minor, not to mention still under contract to a party in Herkimer, Weill had struck a chord with the Herkimer hopeful. Both were optimistic about their future together, which contractually would begin in 1934.[19]

Rated fifth among lightweights by the N.B.A., Lou Ambers was now being compared to Benny Leonard and Jimmy Wilde. Talk about difficult shoes to fill, Leonard, who ended his comeback last year, fought in over 200 battles and only lost five, and Wilde fought nearly 150 times with only three defeats. It was too early, according to most, to make such comparisons, but the youngster was clearly impressing everyone who crossed his path. And, yes, he too was moved by his rapid ascension in the rankings.

The Year in Boxing—1933

It was a peculiar year for boxing, as success was often tampered by remorse. Starting with the success: The month of February saw Battling Shaw, aka José Flores Pérez, capture the world junior welterweight title with a ten-round decision over Johnny Jadick in New Orleans, and Young Corbett III grab the world welterweight title, by defeating Jackie Fields by a ten-round decision in San Francisco.

In May, Tony Canzoneri regained his world junior welterweight title with a ten-round decision over Battling Shaw in New Orleans. "Canzi" looked unbeatable, but he was not. In June, as was noted, Barney Ross beat Tony Canzoneri to claim both the world lightweight and junior welterweight titles held by the New York boxer. It was a ten-round decision held in Chicago. Also, in June, Primo Carnera knocked out heavyweight world champion Jack Sharkey in six rounds at New York City.

In September, Barney Ross retained his world lightweight and junior welterweight titles with a 15-round decision over Tony Canzoneri at New York. Ross had "Canzi's" number and he knew it.

In October, Paulino Uzcudun lost a 15-round decision to Primo Carnera in Rome, Italy. Uzcudun was attempting to become the first Hispanic world heavyweight champion.

And, in December, as noted, Frankie Klick took the world junior lightweight title by knocking out world champion Kid Chocolate, in seven rounds, at Philadelphia.

Also, promoter Jack Dempsey grossed over $200,000 with his "Battle of the Maxes" (Baer & Schmeling); Tommy Loughran, Maxie Rosenbloom and middleweight champion Vince Dundee continued to impress, and few failed to notice that boxers were getting bigger, i.e., Carnera and Ray Impellittiere (aka Ray Impelletiere).

As for the remorse: In addition to the losses by those previously mentioned, there were greater tragedies. Ernie Schaaf died of a brain hemorrhage following his bout with Primo Carnera; furthermore, a punch from his battle with Max Baer, not to mention the flu, may also have contributed. And, William L. Stribling, Jr., aka Young Stribling, died as a result of injuries suffered during a motorcycle accident.